Our Government

The U.S. Constitution

by Christine Peterson

Consultant:
Philip Bigler, Director
The James Madison Center
Harrisonburg, Virginia

Mankato, Minnesota

First Facts is published by Capstone Press,
151 Good Counsel Drive, P.O. Box 669, Mankato, Minnesota 56002.
www.capstonepress.com

Library of Congress Cataloging-in-Publication Data
Peterson, Christine, 1961–
    The U.S. Constitution / by Christine Peterson.
    p. cm.— (First facts. Our government)
    Includes bibliographical references and index.
    ISBN-13: 978-0-7368-9595-8 (hardcover)
    ISBN-10: 0-7368-9595-7 (hardcover)
    ISBN-13: 978-0-7368-7512-7 (softcover pbk.)
    ISBN-10: 0-7368-7512-3 (softcover pbk.)
    1. United States. Constitution—Juvenile literature. 2. Constitutional history—United States—
Juvenile literature. I. Title. II. Series.
E303.P47 2007
342.7302'9—dc22   2006004853

Summary: Describes the U.S. Constitution, its history, and significance.

Editorial Credits
Mandy Robbins, editor; Linda Clavel, designer; Deirdre Barton, photo researcher/photo editor

Photo Credits
Capstone Press/Karon Dubke, 21
Comstock Images, 17
Corbis/Bettmann, cover, 4–5, 6, 10–11, 14–15; Brooks Kraft, 18–19; Richard T. Nowitz, 20
Getty Images Inc./MPI, 7, 8–9, 13; Stock Montage, 17 (top right)

1 2 3 4 5 6 11 10 09 08 07 06

Table of Contents

A Historic Document

In 1787, most countries were ruled by kings and queens. The new U.S. government was an experiment. Americans wrote a **constitution**. It created a government where people could vote for their leaders. The American experiment has lasted more than 200 years.

Fun Fact!
Of all written constitutions, the U.S. Constitution is the oldest and the shortest.

Independence

In the 1700s, Great Britain ruled the American colonies. Britain passed laws many colonists thought were unfair. In 1775, the Revolutionary War broke out.

By July 4, 1776, Americans had declared independence. Soon after, they passed the Articles of Confederation. These rules formed a nation of powerful states.

The New Nation Struggles

Under the command of George Washington, the United States won the war. But the country struggled with the new government.

States were like separate countries. They passed their own laws about trade and taxes. National government had little control.

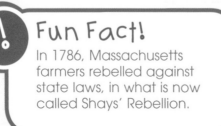

Fun Fact!
In 1786, Massachusetts farmers rebelled against state laws, in what is now called Shays' Rebellion.

James Madison

James Madison is known as the "Father of the Constitution." A lawmaker from Virginia, Madison's plan for the U.S. government was called the Virginia Plan.

After the Philadelphia Convention, Madison served in Congress. He also wrote the Bill of Rights. In 1809, Madison became the fourth president.

Philadelphia Convention

Between May and September of 1787, **delegates** from 12 states met in Philadelphia. They decided to form a new national government.

James Madison had a plan for this government. It included a president to lead the country. A **legislature** would make laws. A **judicial** branch would enforce the laws.

The Great Compromise

But how many people would each state have in the legislature? Delegates from states with more people wanted more representatives. Those from smaller states wanted an equal number.

By July, the delegates compromised. They split the legislature into two parts. The Senate had two representatives from each state. But the number in the House of Representatives was based on population.

Fun Fact!
The Great Compromise passed by just one vote.

A New Government

On September 17, 1787, 39 delegates signed the Constitution. Now it had to be approved by at least nine states.

But not everyone wanted a new government. It took some convincing, but 10 states eventually approved the Constitution. By June 1788, the new government was law.

Federalist Papers

After the Philadelphia Convention, John Jay, Alexander Hamilton, and James Madison wrote 85 letters in favor of the Constitution. These letters became known as the Federalist Papers.

The Federalist Papers were printed in newspapers across the country. They helped the Constitution gain approval from states.

Bill of Rights

The Constitution gave Americans the right to vote for their leaders. But many people thought it should protect other freedoms too. In 1789, Congress agreed to add to the Constitution.

By 1791, the states had voted to add 10 **amendments** to the Constitution called the Bill of Rights. The Bill of Rights protects the freedom of speech, religion, and many other rights.

Fun Fact!

At age 81, Benjamin Franklin was the oldest delegate to sign the Constitution.

CONGRESS, JULY 4, 1776

States of Ame

17

A Living Document

The U.S. Constitution has continued to change along with its people. Since the Bill of Rights, 17 more amendments have been added to the Constitution.

The Constitution still protects Americans' rights today. Its laws guide the president, U.S. leaders, and all Americans.

How do you protect a 200-year-old piece of paper? With bulletproof glass, steel, and concrete. That's how the National Archives protects the Constitution in Washington, D.C.

Each day, hundreds of people view two pages of the yellowed document under bulletproof glass. Each night, the pages are plunged 20 feet (6 meters) underground into a steel and concrete safe. Heavy metal doors cover the safe. Even bombs can't break through them.

Hands On: Make a Bill of Rights

According to the Bill of Rights, certain rights are protected by law. These amendments to the Constitution make sure people are treated fairly. Make your own Bill of Rights for your home or classroom.

What You Need
a group of friends
pen
paper

What You Do

1. Write down what rights are important to you. Do you want the right to share your opinions at home or school? Is privacy important to you?
2. Have your friends do the same.
3. Have each person talk about their rights.
4. Vote on which rights are most important to the group.
5. The five ideas that get the most votes will become your Bill of Rights.
6. Write down your new Bill of Rights.
7. Have everyone sign the Bill of Rights.
8. Display the Bill of Rights at home or in school.

Glossary

amendment (uh-MEND-muhnt)—a change made to a law or a legal document

constitution (kon-stuh-TOO-shuhn)—the written system of laws in a country that state the rights of the people and the powers of the government

delegate (DEHL-uh-geht)—a person who represents other people at a convention

judicial (joo-DISH-uhl)—the branch of government that includes courts; the judicial branch explains laws.

legislature (LEJ-iss-lay-chur)—the branch of government that passes bills that become laws

Read More

Graves, Kerry A. *The Constitution: The Story Behind America's Governing Document.* America in Words and Song. Philadelphia: Chelsea Clubhouse, 2004.

Hamilton, John. *The Constitution.* Government in Action! Edina, Minn.: Abdo, 2005.

Randolph, Joanne. *What is the U.S. Constitution?* New York: Rosen, 2003.

Internet Sites

FactHound offers a safe, fun way to find Internet sites related to this book. All of the sites on FactHound have been researched by our staff.

Here's how:

1. Visit *www.facthound.com*

2. Choose your grade level.

3. Type in this book ID **0736895957** for age-appropriate sites. You may also browse subjects by clicking on letters, or by clicking on pictures and words.

4. Click on the **Fetch It** button.

FactHound will fetch the best sites for you!

Index